A Mouthful of Beans

Once upon a time in a cozy little house, there lived a curious boy named Oliver. Oliver loved eating green beans.

He just couldn't resist stuffing handfuls
of them into his mouth at every meal.

His mom would always say, "Oliver, don't stuff your mouth so full!"

But Oliver paid no attention at all.

A Strange Change

One afternoon, as Oliver was overeating on a heaping plate of green beans, something strange happened.

Green Beans started growing instead of hair! They sprouted from his head and his ears.

Oliver looked like a walking garden!

The Lesson from Mom

Oliver ran to his mom in a panic.

She took one look at her son, covered in greenery, and gently scolded, "There was a reason I told you not to stuff your mouth like that. Oliver! Now you have green bean bushes growing out of you."

The Awakening

With tears in his eyes, Oliver promised to be more careful.

He closed his eyes and hoped for it to be over. So, he went off to bed and of course he dreamed of eating green beans again.

When he opened his eyes, Oliver was
back in his bed.

Oliver's face and hair were free from green beans. It had all been a dream!

A Change in Oliver

From that day forward, Oliver learned to slow down and not to rush his meals.

He enjoyed his green beans just one bite at a time.

Now, he learned to appreciate the wonderful flavor.

And every time he saw a green bean, he couldn't help but smile, remembering his peculiar dream.

Oliver's Mom was very glad that it was only a dream too.

Oliver decided to try another vegetable too! He tried a lot of them!

He even tasted a squash and a cucumber.

Oliver decided he would always eat slow and enjoy his vegetables.

And Oliver planted a garden.

Oliver's favorite vegetable will always be green beans.

Made in the USA
Coppell, TX
04 November 2023

23802727R00017